ARTHUR RANSOME

ARTHUR RANSOME
(*Courtesy of George Newnes Ltd*)

Arthur Ransome

A WALCK MONOGRAPH

by

Hugh Shelley

HENRY Z. WALCK, INCORPORATED
NEW YORK

Library of Congress Catalog Card Number: 64-20836
© The Bodley Head Ltd 1960
First American Edition 1964
Printed in Great Britain

CONTENTS

Acknowledgments, 6

I. The Holidays, 7

II. The Swallows, 13

III. Characters and Character, 18

IV. The First Two, 23

V. Forerunners, Fairy Tales and
Fantasy, 31

VI. Children with Adults, 38

VII. Pigeon Post, 42

VIII. Far Adventure, 48

IX. Illustrations, 55

X. Critics and Buyers, 59

XI. Children and the Writer, 64

Bibliography, 71

58202

ACKNOWLEDGMENTS

I should like to thank Dr Ransome himself, his publishers Jonathan Cape Ltd, and Mrs Robert Stevens for their kindness in providing so much of the material for this monograph; and Mr Anthony Rota for his invaluable help with the bibliography.

HUGH SHELLEY

1. The Holidays

There is a convention about monographs that they should be not merely objective but quite impersonal. Yet there can surely be no valid reason why 'a treatise embodying results of investigation of a single subject' should not be extremely personal; necessarily so in my own case, I submit, when the monograph concerns the books of Arthur Ransome.

Swallows and Amazons was first published in 1930. I was ten in the summer of that year—half way between the eldest and youngest active Swallow. It also happens that my father was a sailor, at that time a Commander in destroyers stationed in Malta; so was the Swallows' father—also a Commander, also out in Malta—the redoubtable Commander Walker, who sent his family a certain cable that altered the whole nature of their school holidays. School holidays, summer holidays; my life, like that of John, Susan, Titty and Roger Walker, centred round them.

Yet until Arthur Ransome, at the age of forty-six, wrote that now famous book that changed the course of so much children's literature, no one had treated school holidays as more than the setting of a novel. As Roger Lancelyn Green says[1],

'there had been many stories of young people's holiday adventures before the coming of *Swallows and*

[1] *Tellers of Tales*, rev. ed. 1953.

Amazons, but usually these were humorous or mischie-
vous or rather staid and serious.'

There had been on the serious side Mrs Molesworth's
The House that Grew and, later, E. Nesbit's books. The
latter were perhaps the true forerunners of Arthur
Ransome's—certainly they were the first about children's life in the holidays to be written with some zest
and humour—and it is interesting to learn that Arthur
Ransome has singled their author out as the only
writer of children's books he can remember reading as a
boy . . . other than Robert Louis Stevenson. Oddly
enough, the very first children's novel to be written
with the object of entertaining rather than instructing
the reader was Catherine Sinclair's *Holiday House*,
published as far back as 1839, but it would be an unusual
child who today could be passionately interested in her
'normal' children, beside whom Mrs Molesworth's
appear young limbs of Satan.

Perhaps school holidays were not so important then.
Certainly they were not for the middle-class girls, who
stayed at home all the year round with a governess. So
despite the fact that one of the Sitwells once claimed to
have been educated 'in the holidays from Eton', it is the
last fifty years that have seen the real growth of the
school holidays as the focal point of English children's
interest.

The reason why Arthur Ransome has become the
Holidays' champion and chronicler is a very simple one;

he has spent the greater part of his seventy-five years either looking forward to, enjoying or looking nostalgically back at them. That is mainly because he is a countryman whose profession alone has brought him to live at times in towns.

The Ransomes were first millers, then agricultural engineers in East Anglia, but Arthur Ransome's great-grandfather was a surgeon (and one of the founders of the Manchester Medical School); his grandfather, a not very successful scientist-inventor, but a first-rate field naturalist, and his father, Professor of History at Leeds. Arthur Ransome, after the death of his father, was sent to school at Rugby, which he left to work in a publisher's office in London.

He admits that he had always lived for his holidays, and they have almost always been spent—as have his happiest years as a writer—in the Lake District, among the hills and becks and tarns, and beside Lake Windermere itself, scene of the early exploits of his Swallows and Amazons. He remembers how as a small boy, the moment he and his family arrived at the farmhouse where they spent their holiday, he would run down to the lakeside and, in ritual, plunge his hands into the water.

Second in his affections is East Anglia, scene of four of his books, where he lived for some years between the two wars—simply because he was unwell and unable to roam the seven seas as he would infinitely have preferred. After all, he had sailed the Baltic in his own boat, and as a correspondent first of the *Daily News* and then of the *Manchester Guardian* he had paid several visits to Russia before, during, and after the Revolution, and had travelled in China, Egypt and the Sudan. However, he was nearly as happy in East Anglia as he had been in the Lake District, for he could still sail—on the Broads and round the coasts of Norfolk and Suffolk— and he could still pursue his other most dear occupation, fishing.

Inevitably then, Arthur Ransome's holidays have been by water. And it will be plain to those least familiar with his books that he has never been really happy out of a boat. The last adult book he wrote before beginning the saga of the Swallows and the Amazons was '*Racondra's*' *First Cruise*, the story of his sailing the Baltic in a boat he had built on its shores, in the years immediately following the first world war. That curiously fascinating book does not really come within the scope of this monograph, which concerns his books specifically published (I will not say written) for children, but it should certainly appeal to many boys in their early teens, and it is of interest to the adult reader of the 'children's' books for the light it throws on its author's views on life in, out of and all around and about boats. It begins,

'Houses are but badly built boats so firmly aground that you cannot think of moving them. They are definitely inferior things, belonging to the vegetable not the animal world, rooted and stationary, incapable of gay transition.'

And Arthur Ransome's literary transitions, the transitions of all the boats in his books, *Swallow* and *Amazon*, *Death-and-Glory* and *Titmouse*, *Wild Cat* and *Shining Moon*, *Sea Bear* and *Goblin*, are fundamentally gay.

'The desire to build a house is the tired wish of a man content thenceforward with a single anchorage. The desire to build a boat is the desire of youth, unwilling yet to accept the idea of a final resting place.'

I have met Arthur Ransome at only two periods of his life, and both of them late. The first was some eight years ago when he blew in to the bookshop I had with a friend in Littlehampton. I say 'blew in' advisedly, for he was in full sail under a voluminous oilskin, a nautical Chesterton. And he had come down to Littlehampton because, within hailing distance of seventy, he was building yet another boat. The next time I saw him was a year ago, when an accident bound him to London, and he could not return to the Lake District. Yet even in London he was by water. His windows overlooked the Thames at Putney, where small boys in canoes, small boys fishing and large men in coracles little knew under what accurate observation they messed about in boats.

From boats, he turns, as a *pis aller*, to camping. Boats come into all the books, but there are regrettable if unavoidable occasions when they are laid up and their sailors cannot be waterborne all summer. The only alternative to the ignominy of ordinary life, 'civilised' life, or as the children so happily call it, 'native' life, is to have canvas rather than plaster and slate between themselves and the sky. And, as in *The Picts and the Martyrs*, even a deserted stone hut proved better than a four-square modern residence with all the usual comforts, sit-down meals and the wrong sort of aunt.

We have established one thing at least: not just holidays but the right sort of holidays are the setting and in great part the substance of Arthur Ransome's books.

II. The Swallows.

Arthur Ransome's twelve books 'for children' are really twelve volumes of one major work, as are the novels that compose the Forsyte Saga or the Dolittle Books. The holidays they chronicle are consecutive and the Swallows and Amazons of the first volumes appear, sometimes separately, sometimes together, in most of the others. The Swallows, as I have mentioned, are the Walker Family, who are allowed to use the little sailing dinghy, *Swallow*. They appear in nine of the volumes, while their rivals and friends, Nancy and Peggy Blackett, who own the *Amazon*, also appear in nine. The two books in which neither family appears, *Coot Club* and *The Big Six*, set on the Norfolk Broads, both feature 'the 2 D's', Dick and Dorothea Callum, who are later friends of the Swallows and the Amazons, and share their adventures in four of the other books.

The children grow naturally older volume by volume, and the (fictional) lapse of time between *Swallows and Amazons* and *Great Northern?* is between five and six years. For this reason, because the author is constantly referring to occasions and characters in previous books, and because both style and subject matter are simplest in the early books, would-be readers are strongly recommended by him and his publishers to begin with Volume 1. Which is what I propose to do in discussing first the heroes and heroines of the saga.

The Walker children arrive with their mother to spend their summer holidays at a farm on the shores of 'the Lake' in the Lake District. It is basically Lake Windermere, but for the purposes of the story it has borrowed one or two features from Lake Coniston—Peel Island, in particular. Peel Island, re-christened Wild Cat Island, is the focal point of *Swallows and Amazons*. Of course it had to be an island, accessible only by boat, and that, for the Walkers, could only mean a sailing boat.

The book opens in classic fashion,

'Roger, aged seven, and no longer the youngest of the family, ran in wide zig-zags, to and fro, across the steep field that sloped up from the lake to Holly Howe, the farm where they were staying for part of the summer holidays. . . . The wind was against him, and he was tacking up against it to the farm, where at the gate his patient mother was awaiting him. He could not run straight against the wind because he was a sailing vessel, a tea-clipper, the *Cutty Sark*.'

Mrs Walker had a telegram form in her hand. It was in answer to her query whether the children, John, Susan, Titty and Roger, should be allowed to sail in *Swallow*, a thirteen-foot dinghy, to Wild Cat Island, and camp there *all by themselves*. The now historic cable she received from her husband, Commander Walker, in Malta, read,

'BETTER DROWNED THAN DUFFERS
IF NOT DUFFERS WONT DROWN'

So the Walkers sat down and composed their ship's articles:

> *Master:* John Walker
> *Mate:* Susan Walker
> *Able-seaman:* Titty Walker
> *Ship's Boy:* Roger'

That was in the summer of 1930. And for the next seventeen years (in the telling—as opposed to the five or six years of the saga's own chronology) they are still the Master, or Captain; the Mate; the Able-seaman and the Ship's Boy. And hundreds of thousands of children will have played their parts, including, apparently, H.M. the Queen. Louis Wulff, in an article entitled 'These Books are Royal Favourites'[1], has written,

> 'Both Princess Elizabeth and her sister have an inbred love of boats and the sea, and as youthful Sea Rangers of the crew of the *Duke of York*, their "ship" at Windsor Castle, have often repeated, at least in imagination, some of the daring exploits of the Swallows and the Amazons.'

Who *are* the book's children? Did they really exist? Are their prototypes now middle-aged mariners? Apparently the reading public still believes that novelists' characters are invariably drawn from life. Only a year ago, Arthur Ransome received a letter from

[1] *Daily Mail Ideal Home Book.* 1949-50, p. 237.

a university lecturer asking if (the supposed original of) Commander Walker ' "really" sent that cable'.

There does indeed exist a family of four sisters and a brother, who are intimately connected with the saga. They are all now grown up and married, they are extremely fond of Arthur Ransome, and their own children—most, if not all fifteen of them—now camp on Peel *alias* Wild Cat Island. It is to these five that *Swallows and Amazons* is dedicated—'in exchange for a pair of slippers'.

It is not, however, true, as many people have imagined, that Arthur Ransome wrote his first book *about* this family. He had already written the greater part of *Swallows and Amazons* before getting to know the five children at all intimately. True, he had known their parents well when he himself was a young man, but he had met the children only by chance and casually until a certain day.

Arthur Ransome was living and writing in his cottage on the shore of Lake Windermere and understandably resented the frequent intrusion of friends arriving in the district for their holidays and expecting him to relax with them when he wanted to get on with his work. He had in fact warned the children's father to stay away, and when one morning he saw his motor car outside the house, Arthur Ransome stormed out to berate him. On reaching the gate, however, he discovered that his disturber had armed himself with a shield. He was pushing in front of him two small girls bearing as a peace offering—a pair of carpet slippers. Utterly disarmed, Arthur Ransome capitulated. And soon he was changing the names of his Swallows to those they now bear, and altering some of the circumstances of the story to make it seem possible for the real children to feel they were the originals of his heroes and heroines.

As the now grown-up John says, not one single adventure in any of the books sprang from anywhere but its author's imagination; only incidentals were taken from life. And there were no 'originals' of the Amazons, Nancy and Peggy Blackett, though Arthur Ransome does remember a sudden glimpse he once had when sailing on the Lake of two little girls in identical red woollen hats sitting on the bank.

It is satisfactory to be able to scotch so demonstrably the myth of 'originals', for it shows that both Swallows and Amazons, like all characters of stature, are entirely their author's creatures and yet become more real to the dedicated reader than his or her closest friend. And Arthur Ransome, in common with other authors, is far more pleased and flattered to learn that young readers have taken his characters to their hearts than that they are thrilled by the plot or entranced by the setting.

III. Characters and Character

It is Arthur Ransome's triumph that both the scenes and characters of his books become so real to their readers, that people insist that there must have been models for both. Indeed, Arthur Ransome has written,

'I know the geography of the country in the books so well that when I walk about in actual fact, it sometimes seems to me that some giant or earthquake has been doing a little scene shifting overnight.'[1]

His characters are even more lifelike, lively and memorable. The Amazons, who are not mere visiting holiday-makers like the Swallows but actually have the luck to live on the shores of the Lake, are Nancy and Peggy Blackett. Peggy is a normally healthy and sporting girl, but she shrinks to an insignificant, docile pawn, with neither mind nor will of her own beside her outrageous elder sister. Nancy is the tomboy of tomboys, the utterly uninhibited leader, whom all the others follow without question, the complete extrovert, who leaves her contemporaries and her elders breathless and speechless.

' "Jib-booms and bobstays!" shouted Nancy Blackett, violently wrestling with a screw in one of her skates. "Nobody could beat those signals." '

The above quotation from *Winter Holiday* exemplifies

[1] *Junior Bookshelf*, Vol I, 4 (A letter to the Editor).

her defeating enthusiasm and energy. She could belong to no other sex, nation or background.

' "*Mille millions de sabords!*" the French translator makes her exclaim, "*tout en battant avec un des écrous de ses patins, ces signaux sont tout simplement formidables.*" '

Somehow, it just doesn't ring true! And as Nancy cannot be translated into a foreign language, so as a character one feels she could not be transmuted into a satisfactory, normal adult. One of Arthur Ransome's correspondents amused herself trying to imagine the future of the Swallows and the Amazons when they grew up. All, she felt, would be happy, with the exception of Nancy. She probably excelled herself in the recent war as a WREN, but afterwards . . . ? No, it is best to think of her for ever on the brink of her teens, at the helm of her ship, ever enthusiastic, resourceful and defiant.

The second strongest character of the books, and he, too, makes his appearance in the first, is, oddly enough, an adult. This is the Blacketts' idiosyncratic Uncle Jim, re-christened by the Walkers, 'Captain Flint', for they believe him to be a retired pirate. His is to no small extent a self-portrait. He is large and rather bald and disguised only by the absence of his creator's very fine (and once piratical) moustache. He is a rover, a sailor, a writer, an angler and a would-be solitary. Being irascible by nature, and certainly no besotted child lover, he is extremely put out when he is led to believe that the young are deliberately annoying him. This is one of the principal themes of *Swallows and Amazons*. Uncle Jim grossly misjudges the Swallows and is despicably unfair to them. When he discovers his mistake, he is immediately and most honourably remorseful, makes the fullest, most generous amends, and from that minute on becomes an honorary uncle to the Walkers and is the only adult allowed to share their and the Blacketts' adventures in subsequent books. Amiable, omniscient bachelor uncles on the side of the children rather than of their parents, have long been commonplaces of children's fiction. But Uncle Jim is the doyen of them all, besides being by far the most convincing.

While Nancy is the moving spirit behind the Swallows' and Amazons' adventures, and Uncle Jim their benevolent and beneficent supporter, who can give the sanction and aid without which parental opposition would scotch their plans, it is the Walkers who are the real heroes of the saga, with whom the reader must identify him- (or her-) self. It is more than an incidental pleasure to discover that Arthur Ransome, unlike the majority of his contemporaries writing for children, does not pander to the ten-year-old's article of faith that all females, bar 'sporting' mothers and aunts, are inexcusable interlopers in a world created by Dr Arnold.

The eldest Walker, Captain John, is their serious-minded leader. He is a thoroughly nice boy, who is determined to be a credit to his father and is the most nautically minded and knowledgeable of the five. It is a slight surprise to find him still at school in his teens and not at Dartmouth. The eldest girl, Mate Susan, is the domestically-minded one who sees to it that the others have enough to eat and wear, and, if they get their feet wet, change their socks or put on their plimsolls. She is almost a Native, as the children call the adults. The next girl, Titty, is a complete contrast. Although she is anxious to be as good a sailor as John, and could not bear anyone to think her feeble, she is by nature an unpracticable dreamer (to those who despise her) or, as her family and friends happily admit, the only one with a properly developed imagination and sensibility. She sees dangers that the others ignore, and yet she conquers a natural timidity far stronger than theirs to help overcome them. Roger, the youngest active Swallow, until *Secret Water*, when Bridget joins the party, is—again by contrast—an amiably simple character. He thinks of only two things: engines (he refuses to kotow to his brother's and sisters' god of canvas) and food. The latter, whether it be the next meal, snack or bar of chocolate.

There are two other major characters, but they do not appear until the fourth volume, *Winter Holiday*, where they join forces with the Walkers and the Blacketts. These are Dick and Dorothea Callum. She is a literary romantic and a writer, at first slightly despised, or at any rate disregarded by the Swallows and Amazons, but finally accepted for her courageous support of what to most children would be a freak of a brother. Dick is studiously scientific, 'a swot', in the eyes of his generation. It is to Arthur Ransome's very great credit that, as another critic has already remarked, Dick never degenerates into a clown. He could so easily have become the buffoon of the party. Instead, the peaceable Roger is only too ready to be laughed at for his concentration on what at that era was a 'tuppenny bar', while Dick, in the very last book, the last volume of the saga, *Great Northern?*, becomes the acknowledged hero, and—even Nancy tacitly admits it—the real leader of them all.

Those readers for whom this short monograph is their first introduction to the name of Ransome may well be puzzled at such emphasis on the characters in his books, when their content has been discussed only in very general terms. However, so many reviewers and critics have praised the books primarily for their plots that people forget that the distinction of Arthur Ransome as a writer for children lies not in telling 'rattling good yarns' and becoming a twentieth-century Ballantyne, but in his ability to write about children who were not only credible, attractive individuals who grew up as they grew older, but also personalities with whom at least a million children have been able to identify themselves. In subsequent chapters we can consider the plots and substance of all the twelve volumes, but always in connection with the principals and the supporting cast.

IV. The First Two

Swallows and Amazons is not the most professional of the twelve books, but in many ways it is the most endearing, the friendliest. Re-reading it as an adult, one senses the enjoyment and the enthusiastic application with which it was written. For great children's books, unlike the majority of great books for adults, have had joy in—at any rate in the early stages—their making. Lewis Carroll would have enjoyed at least the first telling of Alice's adventures; Kenneth Grahame would have delighted in his letters to 'Mouse'. And as these tales would have been a relaxation to the former after his mathematical text books and to the latter after the daily business of the Bank of England, so the composition of *Swallows and Amazons* must have been a delight after a score of books of essays, literary criticism and history, and political studies of the U.S.S.R. and China, for Arthur Ransome, as I shall mention in more detail later, was a professional writer for *a quarter of a century* before he wrote his first book that made his name as a writer for children.

The Swallows, as I have explained, land on Wild Cat Island. The grown-ups, the Natives, are satisfactorily cut off and unable to interfere, and so the children are free to do exactly as they wish. But whereas a lesser writer would have plunged straightway into action and adventure, this leisurely tyro among children's writers is quite content to let his Swallows explore the island, set up camp, eat and drink, swim and fish for four whole chapters.

When adventure comes, it is in the very tame form of the arrival of the Amazons. A brief skirmish, a parley, and Swallows and Amazons take to each other and make a treaty. It is lucky they do, for the Blacketts' Uncle Jim, Captain Flint, is under the misapprehension that the Walkers have been raiding the ancient pleasure steamer turned houseboat in which he periodically lives and tries to work. The true villains had been his own nieces, who had thrown fireworks on to the old hulk's roof, angered by their uncle's recent withdrawal into Native life. Soon, however, real thieves board and break into the houseboat. They steal the only object that looks as though it might contain valuables, an old tin trunk. The contents, however, are neither money nor jewels, but the manuscript of Uncle Jim's book of reminiscences. It is rediscovered thanks entirely to Titty—the over-imaginative Titty, who, when Swallows and Amazons plan a mock battle, overcomes her fear of being left alone on the island, manages to capture the *Amazon*, and spending the night in her off a deserted shore hears the sounds of men burying something. The rediscovery of the trunk and manuscript crowns a reconciliation with Uncle Jim, who makes up for ill-natured, unjustified mistrust of the Swallows by organising a grand finale of a battle: Swallows and Amazons *versus* the Houseboat, boarding it in approved piratical fashion and making its captain actually walk

24

the plank. The summer holidays are over and, one perfect late summer evening, the *Swallow* sails back to civilisation, her crew all singing,

> 'Oh, soon we'll hear the Old Man say,
> "Leave her, Johnny, leave her." '

until land and Natives heave in sight once more.

' "Who *was* Johnny?" said Roger. "Hullo, there's mother and Vicky coming down the field." '

*   *   *

The successor and sequel to *Swallows and Amazons* is *Swallowdale*, and what a worthy, satisfying sequel it is. It has the same endearing quality, the same characters and the same setting; it is better written and more exciting.

It is longer too, and by today's standards exceptionally so. Indeed, returning to Ransome after reading more recent children's books, one is struck by the length of his stories. Admittedly, *Swallowdale* is the longest, nearly 150,000 words, but they are all long. Whereas nowadays a children's novel of 60,000 words is quite usual, the shortest Ransome, *The Picts and the Martyrs*, is 64,000 and the average is nearly 90,000. It is astonishing to think that they came out at 7s 6d, (with an average of 26 full-page illustrations and countless tailpieces) and that today each costs only 13s 6d.

The period of *Swallowdale* is the Walkers' second summer in the Lake District, the very next year after their adventures in *Swallow* and *Amazon* and on Wild Cat Island. Roger is now eight; the baby, Vicky, is a toddler and henceforth known by her proper name of Bridget; and they are all much more sure of themselves. Too sure, alas, for right at the beginning of the holidays the Swallows are racing the Amazons, when John fails to reef, and runs *Swallow* on Pike rock, where she is holed and sunk. They manage to salvage her without adult aid, but she is a case for the boatyards, there can be no sailing to the Island this summer; they must find alternative excitement.

Philosophically, they explore the hills, find a Secret Valley and climb 'Kanchenjunga' (the Old Man of Coniston, in geographical fact). And there are many other adventures before *Swallow* is repaired and, in the last two chapters, they are once more racing *Amazon*. The Amazons, incidentally, play a smaller part than hitherto, for they (and poor Uncle Jim as well) have 'native trouble', in the shape of an impossibly pernickety Great Aunt.

Sad though this may be for Nancy's admirers, we do get to know the Walkers far better. By the end of the book they are as familiar as our closest friends, not only because Arthur Ransome identifies himself and makes us identify ourselves with them, but because he takes time over them. As in *Swallows and Amazons*, there is no rush to get on with the story. Pages are spent in describing the daily, even the hourly, life of the children. Susan, at her most 'native', reminds them of their holiday tasks and Titty doggedly takes her French Grammar out one morning.

'She had a pretty firm hold on *J'ai*, *tu as*, *il a* but was still muddled with *avais* and *aviez* and *avaient* and lost hope altogether when it came to *eus*, *eut*, *eûmes* and *eurent*.'

And when Susan cooks, there is a detailed description of the best way to make buttered eggs, or to cook fish in camp. Many girls and boys, one hopes, remember Captain Flint's advice to her in *Swallows and Amazons* that if you want to like cooking, you must make the others wash up.

The other agreeably effective way in which Arthur Ransome brings one to know his characters is by frequent back reference. They are continually remembering, as children do, what happened the last time they were in such-and-such a place or predicament. The children are worth getting to know, because they always behave as children and not as cardboard heroes. The place or predicament is never taken in the children's stride as it usually is in the second-rate adventure story. They are ever new and strange; unfamiliar and little frequented country can be very unnerving to children, and Arthur Ransome knows this well. The Walkers and the Blacketts get tired and hungry and feel lonely as children do. And from time to time, their tiredness, hunger and loneliness are such that only adults can assuage them. How different from those heroes and heroines of Cornish cove mysteries, who can retrieve the school cups, unmask the villain and uncover an international spy ring in twenty-four sleepless, foodless, waterless hours. Arthur Ransome is sufficiently familiar with physical discomfort and the disadvantages of solitude to appreciate two major facts of childhood: achievement in the face of ungauged difficulties and hardships is the most exciting thing; loneliness with neither physical nor moral support is the most daunting. In *Swallows and Amazons*, one of the best passages describes how Titty makes up her mind to stay alone on the Island and play her lone part in the night battle between the Amazon pirates and the crew of the *Swallow* rather than take her mother's offer of a row home to civilisation. In *Swallowdale* it is Titty again, who is left alone, this time with a frightened Roger, when the two of them lose their way on the moors in the fog. Roger sprains his ankle—and they have eaten the last of the chocolate. The blackest moment is pictured thus,

' "We must have gone an awful long way to the right," said the Boy.

"It can't be much farther now," said the Able-seaman.

And then, suddenly, their cheerfulness came to an end.

"Look," said Roger, who was a yard or two ahead, "there's a tree! On the other side. I'm going to cross."

"There aren't any trees," said Titty.

"I can see it. It's a big one," said Roger, and jumped.

He landed with a short squeak of pain on the other side. His left foot slipped between two stones and twisted over. He fell forward, tried to pick himself up, squeaked again and flopped on the ground.

"Have you hurt yourself?" asked Titty, jumping across the stream.

"Rather," said the Boy.

"Badly?"

"Very badly. I can't get up. But I was right about the tree. Look at it."

If Roger had something in his mind, nothing would stop him from talking of it. He had been thinking of the tree before he jumped. He was thinking of it still, as he lay beside the stream. Titty looked up.

Close above them a tall pine towered like a grey ghost in the white mist. Titty was almost as much troubled by the tree as by Roger.

"There are no trees on top of the moor," she said. "There aren't any till down on the other side of Swallowdale in the wood above Swainson's Farm."

"Well, there it is," said Roger. "Ouch!"

"Where does it hurt?"

"It's my best foot. Broken, I think."

"Oh, Roger."

"And there is no more chocolate." ' '

Roger is occasionally fanciful and often slightly—

—naturally—silly, while Titty is blessed and cursed with the most vivid of imaginations. Both are determined to overcome their several fears. Whenever they are successful, their heroism is in accordance with their age; their achievements are triumphs of their age. They are genuine heroes.

v. Forerunners, Fairy Tales and Fantasy

Before continuing to follow in the Swallows' and Amazons' wake, it is worth stopping to consider how Arthur Ransome, by nature a romantic and by training and upbringing a practical man, by nature imaginative and by profession and often by inclination a factual man, should have come to make his name by writing books that have been welcomed by the young of so many different nations.

How did he become a writer? He has answered this question himself, most pleasingly, in certain interviews with the Press.

'Until I was about eight years old,' he tells us, 'I was a cheerful small boy of action rather than of letters. Then one day we were playing at ships under and on a big dining-room table which had underneath it, in the middle, a heavy iron screw pointing downwards. It was my watch below. My brother or sister was on the bridge, on top of the table, and suddenly raised a shout for "All hands on deck!" I started up, and that big screw under the middle of the table made a most horrible dent in my skull, altered its shape and so, in one moment, changed my character for life. I crawled out, much shaken; and that very afternoon wrote my first book, about a desert island, in a little notebook with a blue cover. I have been writing ever since.'

After leaving his public school, Rugby, he went to

London and worked in a publishing house, becoming an office boy in the firm of Grant Richards. From that insecure bridgehead he made forays into the literary world. By the age of twenty-one, he had published two small volumes of short pieces that had appeared in various periodicals, and in 1907, when he was twenty-three, he wrote *Bohemia in London*, a charming, if occasionally mannered, and nostalgic, almost elderly, book of reminiscences about his own and others' literary life in the capital just three years previously! After editing *The World's Story-tellers* for T. C. & E. C. Jack, he put together for them his first full-length book, *A History of Story-telling*. This paved the way for a study of Edgar Allan Poe and another on Oscar Wilde. Arthur Ransome spent much time in studying the technique of story-telling, and the later books of reportage on China and Russia that he wrote after the war as well as his one book on sailing, '*Racundra*'s' *First Cruise*, and his first collection of fishing articles, *Rod and Line*, gave him experience in writing economically and accurately as well as fluently. It is perhaps worth noting that Arthur Ransome's second collection of fishing essays, *Mainly about Fishing*, which appeared only in February 1959, is every whit as vigorous and delightful as its predecessor published thirty years ago. It is a pleasure to the uninstructed, and evidently to the expert; in the periodical *Angling*, the reviewer remarks that it 'joins the group of books that are read again and again, in whole or part, as long as eyesight lasts.'

As can be seen from the bibliography at the end of this monograph, Arthur Ransome has written many more books for adults that I have not mentioned, and I shall not attempt to discuss the very considerable quantity of his work that has appeared only in periodicals. He also wrote some fairy stories that were, he says, 'as bad as they could be'. There are, however, two children's books outside the Swallow and Amazon saga that are worth consideration. In 1919 appeared his rhymed version of *Aladdin*. After a merrily defiant dedication to Lascelles Abercrombie, he launches out into,

'The wind blows through the bamboo wood,
The coloured lanterns swing and gleam,
And sleeping Chinese children dream
Of small Aladdin and his Djinns.'

It is a handsome crown 4to, with Dulac-like illustrations by Mackenzie; the story is told with despatch and humour in fine, spanking verse, with an occasional surprising subtlety of rhythm; and many parents must have read it to their children with zest. One must admit, however, that it is no landmark in children's literature and Arthur Ransome does not intend to reprint it.

*   *   *

The other book is a very different matter; it has been in print for nearly half a century. *Old Peter's Russian Tales*, first published in 1916, was the result of Arthur Ransome's first visit to Russia. He went there to collect the material for a book of Russian fairy stories, a year before the outbreak of the first world war.

In his Note to the first edition, Arthur Ransome says,

'I think there must be more fairy stories told in Russia than anywhere else in the world. In this book are a few of those I like best. I have taken my own way with them more or less, writing them mostly from memory.'

He had started by trying to translate them direct from the Russian, but discovered that straightforward translations were unsatisfactory; children found them difficult and dull. So he retold them in words which he put into the mouth of an old Russian peasant, Peter, who lives with his two grandchildren in the heart of the forest. The two children, Vanya and Maroosia, ask him to tell them the tales to while away the long winter evenings. The practical details and working of machines and contraptions, gadgets and gilhickies, that are such a feature of the later books are foreshadowed in the detailed description of making tea . . . in a samovar.

The stories themselves are delightfully told and suit Arthur Ransome's taste in humour and for colour and magic. *Baba Yaga*, *The Fire Bird*, *Frost*, *The Fool of the World* and *The Cat who became Head-forester* are some of the twenty-one folk tales in the book that the people of the Russian countryside have passed down to each other for generations.

*   *   *

The two books in the Swallow and Amazon saga that most closely resemble Arthur Ransome's earlier writings are *Peter Duck* and *Missee Lee*. These differ from the other ten books in that they are imaginary adventures supposedly invented by the Swallows and the Amazons to beguile winter evenings between their own summer holiday adventures. They are said to have been told on board a wherry, hired by Uncle Jim for them all to spend their Christmas holidays in on the Norfolk Broads. Their principal creator was naturally made out to be Titty.

Peter Duck, although published in 1932, after *Swallowdale*, was actually planned before it, as observant readers of the latter will have divined. In *Swallowdale* there are several references to Titty's imaginary friend,

'Peter Duck had grown up gradually to be one of the Able-seaman's most constant companions, shared now and then by the Boy, but not taken very seriously by the others, though nobody laughed at him. . . . Peter Duck, who said he had been afloat ever since he was a duckling, was the old sailor who had voyaged with them to the Caribbees in the story and, still in the story, had come back to Lowestoft with his pockets full of pirate gold.'

After seeing the photograph in *'Racundra's' First Cruise*, one feels that he must to some extent have been based on 'The Ancient Mariner', the classic (Baltic) old salt, who crew'd for Arthur Ransome on that voyage, while his wife grappled with the galley.

Both *Peter Duck* and *Missee Lee* give Arthur Ransome full opportunity to indulge his taste for credibly outrageous fantasy. In *Peter Duck*, Captain Flint takes the Walkers, the Blacketts and the aforementioned 'ancient' to the Caribbean, racing the scoundrelly Black Jake and his crew aboard the *Viper* for the treasure buried in Crab Island. In *Missee Lee*, they sail out of their hundredth port and into trouble in the China Sea; they are captured by a superbly logical, implacable and highly cultured pirate captain: Missee Lee herself. (After mentioning the samovar in *Old Peter's Russian Tales*, it would be a pity not to note the tailpiece to Chapter IX. It is entitled, 'How to eat with chopsticks'.)

The originality of *Peter Duck* and *Missee Lee* compared with the bulk of fantasies for the young lies, paradoxically, in their factual approach. Often they are more concerned with the mechanics of 'going foreign' than are the 'true' stories of the Swallows and the Amazons with the technicalities of sailing. *Peter Duck*, for example, contains detailed drawings of the ship in which they sail to the Caribbean, and Arthur Ransome tells how he carefully worked out the course from Lowestoft to 'Crab Island' so that the adventurous could actually sail there and back with the aid of the text and the end-paper map. As for *Missee Lee*, the author visited China and wrote a book about it, *Chinese Puzzle*, after being sent out there by the *Manchester Guardian* at the time of the Chinese Revolution.

Even more striking than the accuracy of the background is the consistency with which the children, in their own story, the one they made up, behave exactly as they would under the story's circumstances. With a sigh of relief one realises that it would be blowhard Nancy, by all the barbecued billygoats in the northern hemisphere, who was irremediably seasick as the *Wild Cat* lurched south down the North Sea. It is an agreeable surprise that the desperately keen John should be less confident than he was on the Lake. At one point Captain Flint called him to take over the wheel and,

'John gulped, but said "Aye, aye, sir," as stoutly as he could. A moment later he was feeling the ship, meeting her as she yawed, looking anxiously back at her rather waggly wake, and trying to do with a real ship at sea what he had learnt to do very well with the little *Swallow* on the Lake in the North.'

VI. Children with Adults

Personally, I am glad to get back to the Lake in the North, to Coniston-Windermere, as Arthur Ransome's ability to create fantastic reality is to me more exciting than his admittedly remarkable achievement in writing realistic fantasy.

The other books about the Lake are *Winter Holiday*, *Pigeon Post* and *The Picts and the Martyrs*. The first two are early; *Winter Holiday* follows immediately after *Swallowdale* in both factual and fictional time, and only *Coot Club* comes between *Winter Holiday* and *Pigeon Post*. *The Picts and the Martyrs* is the penultimate volume of the twelve and the shortest. It is also, I think, the least successful. Ransomanes are so far united in refusing to criticise any of 'the twelve', but I must risk their giving me the black spot as Nancy memorably gave it to Captain Flint, by suggesting that we are brought back to the Lake—after sorties into strange parts of the British Isles—a little under false pretences. The plot mainly concerns the efforts of the Amazons and the 2 D's to outwit the abominable Great Aunt, whom we had not met since *Swallowdale*. But perhaps I am prejudiced by the absence of the Swallows.

The 2 D's, Dick and Dorothea Callum, first enter the saga in *Winter Holiday*. They happen to be staying at Dixon's farm, so it is inevitable that they should meet the Walkers and the Blacketts, spending their winter holidays respectively at Holly Howe and Beckfoot. As I have mentioned, they are a scientifically minded, very serious boy and his literary younger sister. There is something rather pathetic about their dogged loyalty respectively to fact and fiction and to each other. Both are frightened of being thought duffers and their great ambition is to be approved, or at least to pass muster, by such obviously capable children as the Blacketts and the Walkers.

The Lake is almost as attractive in winter as in summer, particularly as it freezes solid,[1] Nancy goes down with mumps, and as all the rest are in quarantine, the holidays are prolonged. The story is about an expedition they plan to make by sledge to 'the North Pole', the farthest northern shore of the Lake. Captain Flint's houseboat is iced up and becomes the *Fram* (Nansen's ship) acting as the expedition's headquarters until Nancy is well again and they can all set off.

Captain Flint returns unexpectedly from abroad and at once enters into the spirit of the expedition. By now the position of the grown-ups in the stories has become clearly defined. Strangers who merely happen to cross the children's horizon are imagined to be something else that will not spoil the fantasy of their adventures. The skaters on the frozen Lake that has become the Arctic Ocean encasing the *Fram*, are counted as Eskimos or seals, just as in *Swallowdale*, when Titty and Roger went off exploring on their own, the hooting cars on the

[1] As it did in fact when Arthur Ransome, a small boy, was at school at Windermere in the early 'nineties.

main road became trumpeting savages. Adults within the children's family circle become Natives for the purposes of fantasy, but they are acknowledged to have 'real' lives as well. All of them (with the exception of that Great Aunt) are remarkably good-natured and willing to give the children what assistance they can to make the games, adventures and expeditions a success. Uncle Jim is their mainstay, but the others help staunchly. At times, there is an almost feudal atmosphere, for not only parents and other relations join in, but the lower orders[1] play their part. One is forcibly reminded that the first books were written in the early 'thirties, when the middle classes still had servants. However, one feels that the farmers' wives who lodge the children and the various locals they meet are friendly only because they are amused by and like the children. Other characters, such as the two Billies, the charcoal burners who appear in both *Swallows and Amazons* and *Swallowdale*, Mary Swainson in *Swallowdale*, and others, are all pleasant open folk. Their deference is the natural, often protective, politeness of country people. What is more, they are never mere ciphers; they have definite characters, unlike the background yokels of so many children's books. And their dialect, unlike the Mummerset of fictional coastguards, has the ring of authenticity. One of the nicest of Arthur Ransome's Westmorlanders (or northern Lancastrians) is Mr Dixon, the farmer

[1] '*In the Lake country there are no "lower orders"*.'—Arthur Ransome.

who speaks to no one until the Callums appear on the scene, when he and Dick strike up a convincingly odd friendship that astonishes even Mrs Dixon.

On the whole, though, the children's relations with the adult world are a minor matter. It is their relationship with each other and their development that is most interesting. Some, like Susan and Roger, are simple characters, so simple that adult readers may weary of the constant repetition of their not very subtle characteristics. Susan's Native mind, her preoccupation with the domestic economy of each expedition and adventure, its victualling, health and hygiene, is constantly reiterated, while Roger's ever-empty stomach and thoughts of chocolate recur in book after book. But these repetitions are not solely for the sake of opposing Susan's practical to Nancy's adventurous, Dorothea's romantic and Titty's imaginative approach, or, for that matter, of bringing in Roger's unworthy pangs as light relief. Children love repetition, both comic repetition (which, of course, is a basic ingredient of the most primitive comedy) and serious repetition that gives the sense of continuity and security their conservative natures require. If one can remember one's own childhood, it is not hard to understand what the little girl meant when she wrote to Arthur Ransome,

'Please write another book exactly like the last with the same people and the same places and all the same things happening.'

Pigeon Post, sixth of the series, and one of the most complete, is an outstanding example of Arthur Ransome's ability not only to analyse character and show its development but to do so dramatically. And in terms any boy or girl of average sensitivity can appreciate.

Pigeon Post was the first book to win the now famous Carnegie Medal. The Medal was instituted by the Library Association and awarded to Arthur Ransome in 1936, not so much, one is given to understand, for his achievement in *Pigeon Post* itself, but to honour the man who was unquestionably the foremost English children's writer at the time. *Swallows and Amazons*, *Swallowdale*, *Peter Duck*, *Winter Holiday* and *Coot Club* were the books it crowned. Because of this *Pigeon Post* and its successors are often underrated. Not, I am glad to say by all critics. In his *Twentieth Century Children's Books*, Frank Eyre describes it as 'one of his best stories . . . a perfect model of how to write a children's story, for in it he subjects his group of children to all the superficial ingredients of the conventional children's "thriller". There is a mysterious stranger, a search for treasure, midnight excursions and so on; but how skilfully it is all handled and how differently the children themselves react. And yet how much more truly exciting it is than the usual nonsense.'

The 'miners' camp', sought by the 'prospectors', is

threatened from various quarters. First, the Blacketts' mother feels that they are all going too far afield for her to feel happy about them, and this is where the pigeons come in. The children release them at intervals to reassure her that they are all right. Then lack of water makes their chosen camping ground unfeasible and they have to put up their tents in an orchard in the lee of the most civilised of farms. I was in error when I said that all grown-ups bar the Great Aunt were sympathetic. Mrs Tyson is the queen of uncomprehending adult females; instead of leaving them to fend for themselves and cook in their own billycans over their own fires, she prepares admirable sustaining suppers and makes them feel ashamed of being five minutes late for them.

There is only one way out; they *must* find water near their chosen camping site. Hopes are raised when Dick finds rushes that grow only where there is water. If only one of them were a born dowser. . . . They all try with a hazel twig, but it is no good. The irrepressible Roger is fooling around 'discovering' planted jam jars of water, when they realise Titty hasn't had a go. They give her the stick and she sets off.

' "Half a minute," said Captain Nancy eagerly. "Didn't it give a sort of jerk just now?"

Titty looked round miserably. "It can't have," she said.

"There it is again," said Nancy. "Look here. . . ."

Titty's eyes were swimming. She saw the ground of the yard at her feet through a mist. Something queer was happening that she could neither help nor hinder. The stick was more than a bit of wood in her hands. It was coming alive. If only she could drop it, and be free from it. But there was Captain Nancy's voice, talking, close to her and yet far away. . . . The ends of the stick were lifting her thumbs. She fought against them, trying as hard as she could to hold them still. But the fork of the stick was dipping, dipping. Nothing could stop it. Her hands turned in spite of her. "Titty! Titty!" They were all talking to her at once. The next moment the stick had twisted clean out of her hands. It lay on the ground, just a forked hazel twig with the green showing through the bark where Nancy's knife had trimmed it. Titty, the dowser, startled more than she could bear, and shaking with sobs, had bolted up into the wood.'

All the others agree that Titty must not be forced to dowse against her will, but after a dismal day that began with Nancy going out alone to try with the twig—near a little puddle, round which the naturalist Dick had observed the tracks of some small animal—and ended with them all in black despair, Titty slips out after supper by herself.

'She had reached the top of the wood and the turning through the bushes to the old pitstead of the charcoal-burners when she heard a quick rustling of dried leaves and twigs. Something small was coming down to meet her. She pulled out her torch, but did not light it. The thing, whatever it was, was on the path close above her. She stood perfectly still. There it was. A rabbit? No. She knew now what it was that had left the muddy

44

prints by the pool halfway down the hill. Steadily trotting down the path, now and then lifting its head to sniff, a hedgehog came hurrying in the dusk. He seemed to know that something strange was about, but he looked for things of his own height, and never saw Titty, towering above him. He passed close to her feet, carelessly, noisily hurrying down the path as if the wood belonged to him.

"He wants water, too," said Titty to herself. "And he's got to go down the hill for it, just like us. He'd be jolly glad if I did find any near the top."

She let the hedgehog get well below her, so as not to startle him, and then went on to the camp that might have been. There was more light in the open space that the charcoal-burners had cleared. Titty knew just where Nancy had thrown her forked twig in the morning. Nancy would be sure to cut the right twig. It would be better to try with that instead of looking for another.

She found the twig at once and picked it up by the point of the fork, putting off to the very last minute the holding of those two ends in her hands. But perhaps it would not work, anyway.

Titty swallowed once or twice. No one was here to see. No one would ever know if, after all, she could not bring herself to do it.

"Oh, come on," she said to herself. "You've got to. Better get it over."

She turned the twig round and took the two ends, one in each hand just as Nancy had shown her by Mrs Tyson's pump. She found herself breathing very fast.

"Duffer," she said firmly. "You can just drop it if you want."

She began walking to and fro across the level platform of the old fire spot. Nothing happened.

"Idiot," she said. "It won't be here, anyway."

She left the platform and went in among the trees, looking in the dim light for Dick's green rushes. She found a tuft of them. Still nothing happened.

"It's all right," she said to herself. "You can't do it. It was only an accident the other night. Nothing to be afraid of anyway. And you've tried. So it wasn't your fault. . . ."

And then she nearly dropped the twig. There it was, that tickling. Not like the other night at Tyson's. But the same thing. The twig was trying to move.

For a long time she stood where she was, somehow not daring to stir. Then she took a step or two, and the stick was as dead as ever.

"This is silly," she said, and stepped back to the place where she had been and felt the stick press against the balls of her thumbs just as it had before.

"Well, it can't bite you," said Titty, and made herself walk to and fro, among the bushes and low trees at the edge of the wood just as she had on the open platform of Might Have Been.

The twig was moving again. Again it stopped. Again it twitched in her fingers.

"There *is* water here," said Titty to herself. "There must be. Unless it's all rot, like Dick thought."

She walked slowly on. The twig was pulling harder and harder. She wanted to throw it down, but somehow, by herself, she was not as frightened of it as she had been when, all unexpectedly, she had felt it for the first time. No one was watching her now, for one thing. She had won her battle the moment she had brought herself to hold the twig again. Now, already, she was almost eagerly feeling the pulling of the twig. When it weakened she moved back until she felt it strengthen. Then again she walked on. It was like looking for something hidden, while someone, who knew where it was, called out hot or cold as she moved nearer to or farther from the hiding place.

Suddenly, as she came nearer the Great Wall, the twisting of the twig became more violent. Here was a shallow dip in the ground between two rocks, and, yes, there was another tuft of those rushes in the bottom of it. She walked in between the rocks and it was just as it had been in the farmyard at Tyson's. The stick seemed to leap in her hands. The ends of it pressed against her thumbs, while the point of the fork dipped towards the ground, bending the branches, twisting her hands round with them, and at last almost springing out of her fingers.

"It's here," said Titty. "I've found it!" '

VIII. Far Adventure

The first of the 'real' books to be set away from the Lake District—I except *Peter Duck*—is *Coot Club*, which is also the first to feature neither Swallows nor Amazons but only the 2 D's, whom we had just met for the first time in *Winter Holiday*. They go to spend their Easter holidays on the Norfolk Broads, where they meet the Coot Club. This is a local bird protection society consisting of Tom Dudgeon, an East Anglian doctor's son, and the 'Death and Glories', Jo, Pete and Bill, an intriguing trio, the sons of local boat builders. The story mostly concerns the Coot Club's war with a motor-cruiser load of vulgar landlubbers whom Tom Dudgeon cuts adrift from their mooring right on top of a nesting coot.

The 2 D's come to his aid when he is 'outlawed', and courageously put into practice what they have learned of boat-handling. This, of course, equips them for complete participation in future adventures with the expert Walkers and Blacketts.

We Didn't Mean to Go to Sea, the second of the 'non-Lake' books, and the successor to *Pigeon Post*, is the one I suspect Arthur Ransome himself considers his best. Certainly, it is the most exciting. The motto of the book (and an echo of the same phrase in *Pigeon Post*) is a dictum of Commander Walker, Royal Navy,

'Grab a chance and you won't be sorry for a might-have-been.'

48

Arthur Ransome considers that the greatest tribute ever paid to him was Eric Hiscock's adopting this sentence for his motto and having it carved on the beam above the companionway of his *Wanderer III* before setting out in her on his round the world cruise.

The chance is a heaven-sent one for the Swallows to prove themselves in real difficulties and real danger in quite possible circumstances that could lead to disaster if anyone were to panic. Holidaying in East Anglia—Pin Mill and Shotley are the setting—they meet one Jim Brading who has just sailed his cutter, *Goblin*, up round the coast from Dover. He invites them to spend a night aboard, and while he is ashore fetching petrol for the auxiliary, she drags anchor and, in dense fog, with all the Walkers bar Bridget on board, drifts out to sea. She lands up, after a terrifying night, off Flushing—just as she would have done, for Arthur Ransome, with his passion for accuracy, checked the course by sailing his own yacht to Beach End buoy, letting her drift and then following the *Goblin*'s course.

The reality of the book lies, however, not in the plausibility of its plot, but in the naturalness of the children's behaviour, the effect such an experience has on each. As always, the main interest is not in the situation but in the way the boys and girls react to it. There are no phoney heroics. They are sick as cats, Titty, early on, goes below with a splitting headache, Roger—quite naturally—is scared stiff, and Susan, the stolid domesticated Susan, is at one moment in a flood of tears. So one is not surprised that they make it, that they win through—and even rescue a shipwrecked kitten on the way.

At one point in the middle of the night, John realises that they are carrying too much sail. The wind has got up and they are pitching and tossing, but he determinedly inches along the deck to reef. Susan is left at the tiller.

'And then she saw him get to his feet and stand there, swaying with the leaping boat, with his hands on shrouds and halyards.

"John!" Her call was indignant. What on earth was he doing that for?

"John!" Her angry call turned unexpectedly into a call for help. She was going to be sick again. She choked. Something buzzed in her head. Spots dithered before her eyes. Yes. She was going to be sick now, at once. . . . He must come, quick, to take the tiller for her.

"John! . . . *Oh!*" Her call for help turned to a shriek of terror. John was gone. One moment he had been standing on the foredeck, swaying with the motion of the *Goblin*. The next moment he was gone. A clutching hand missing the shrouds . . . the life-line jerking taut. He was gone . . ." '

When John regains the cockpit, he mentions the fact that he thought he heard her call out. Shamefacedly she says that she thought she was going to be sick.

' ". . . and John . . . it's very queer. I don't feel sea-sick any more."

"Good," said John. "Once it's over, you'll probably never be sea-sick again. How's Titty?" '

And that was that.

*   *   *

One might have thought that the subsequent books would be anticlimaxes, particularly as the next one, *Secret Water*, is about nothing more exciting than surveying. Commander Walker has returned from foreign parts—this time from the China station—and has for the first time entered the saga in person in *We Didn't Mean to Go to Sea*. His steamer, casting off from the quay in Flushing Harbour, passed the *Goblin* and he was put aboard just in time to share his children's very much smoother recrossing of the North Sea. He has returned for some well-earned leave in England, and one cannot help commenting that it seems to have been extraordinarily remiss of the Admiralty to have sent him straight from Malta to China without leave. However, it seems more than remiss of them, particularly in peace time, to cancel his leave, at the beginning of *Secret Water* and insist that he take up his new shore appointment at Shotley, forthwith. How right that *Secret Water* should begin,

'The First Lord of the Admiralty was unpopular at Pin Mill.

"I hate him," said Roger, sitting on the foredeck of the *Goblin*, with his legs dangling over the side.

"Who?" said Titty.

"The first of those lords," said Roger.

"We all hate him," said Titty.'

As Commander Walker cannot spend his children's next holidays with them, he takes them off by boat to camp up an unfrequented East Anglian creek (Hamford Water was the original) on what is an island at high water and a mud-encompassed peninsula at low water. The object of the expedition is to chart the area, which they do with the help of the Amazons who come up to join them for *their* holidays, and a new tribe, the Eels. By now all the children are much older, and for the first time, too, Bridget is allowed to join them.

Although the make-believe adventures and one real one, when the three youngest are nearly cut off by the tide, make up the bulk of the book, the greatest interest is in a minor but to the young, most heart-searching question of loyalty to one's own gang in conflict with one's natural inclinations and desires.

The Big Six of the ninth book's title are the 2 D's, Tom Dudgeon and the Death and Glories, all of whom we met in *Coot Club*. This time they act as detectives and set out to discover who has been stealing from craft on the Broads, in order to clear the Death and Glories, who are suspected of being the culprits. This, of all the twelve books, is the nearest to the conventional 'rattling good yarn'; it is a most competent thriller and the Big Six put in some excellent (and scientific) detective work. It has a felicitous ending. In the course of their adventures, the Death and Glories catch a record pike. An elderly fisherman sees it newly stuffed and displayed in a glass case in the parlour of the 'Roaring Donkey'.

' "Are you the boys who caught that fish?" he asked.
"We didn't exactly . . ." began Joe.
"Poor lads," said the old man. "Poor lads. . . . So young and with nothing left to live for."
"Let's go and catch another," said Pete.'

*   *   *

The Great Northern Diver
'nests abroad . . . usually seen solitary.' *Sandars*

'nests in eastern North America, Greenland and Iceland, may nest in the Shetlands, as it is often round these islands all summer, but this has never been proved.' *Coward*

These quotations are the key to *Great Northern?*, the twelfth and last volume, which is as good as any of its predecessors, and some consider it better than any of them. If Arthur Ransome had to rest on his laurels, the publication of this book was surely the best of occasions.

The Swallows, the Amazons, and the 2 D's are sailing round the Hebrides with Uncle Jim. John must be fifteen or sixteen; Roger, eleven or twelve. It is the end of the holidays and they beach their borrowed boat to scrub her before returning her to her owner. Typically, there is a full-page plate of diagrams showing how a boat is supported on 'legs' when deliberately left high and dry by the receding tide. Dick, the naturalist of the party—trained on the Broads by the Coot Club!—makes his momentous discovery of a pair of Great Northern Divers nesting. All Dick wants to do is to take notes and to photograph them, but an unscrupulous professional egg-collector appears on the scene. It takes all the resourcefulness of the Swallows, the Amazons and the 2 D's to outwit him and at the same time to avoid capture themselves by the islanders who suspect that their curious manoeuvres on the island are part of some plan to poach their deer.

The final chase is as excitingly told as any incident in any of the books. Satisfactorily, it is Dick who saves the birds from being shot by the collector and Titty who finds the eggs that the villain had stolen from the nest. Together they put the eggs back in the nest, and the book ends with them watching the two Great Northern Divers return to sit on them.

' "Come on," said Titty. "Let's go and tell the others."

"Gosh! Oh gosh!" said Dick, almost as if he were Roger, and, blinking joyfully through his spectacles, pulled for the shore.'

IX. Illustrations

All twelve of the books are very fully illustrated, with an average of twenty-six full-page plates (*Secret Water* has as many as forty-one), end-paper maps and numerous tailpieces to the chapters. Today, the illustrations must be regarded by many people as an integral part of the saga, yet the first edition of *Swallows and Amazons* contained no pictures at all. The second edition carried end-paper maps by Stephen Spurrier, and illustrations by Clifford Webb. Stephen Spurrier's maps have a nice swashbuckling quality, and Clifford Webb is a fine decorative artist. Why, then, are all the books now 'illustrated' by Arthur Ransome, who states that he cannot draw for toffee? What happened?

The answer is this: when Arthur Ransome wrote *Peter Duck* it struck him very forcibly that as the story was supposed to be written by the Swallows and Amazons themselves, it would add to the book's verisimilitude if they were also supposed to illustrate it. None of them (save, possibly, Titty?) could draw very well, so who better to make their pictures for them than the real author. A note at the beginning of *Peter Duck* states that all the children (even Roger) had a hand in the drawings, and is signed: 'Captain Nancy Blackett'.

Arthur Ransome decided that henceforth he would illustrate all his own books, and furthermore, that he would re-illustrate *Swallows and Amazons* and *Swallowdale*, the first edition of which had also been illustrated by Clifford Webb. The new edition of *Swallowdale* was announced as 'illustrated by the Author with help from Miss Nancy Blackett'; in *Winter Holiday* Arthur Ransome says 'I have to thank Miss Nancy Blackett for much earnest work on the illustrations of this book'; and in *Pigeon Post* he writes, 'As usual I have to thank Miss Nancy Blackett, whose drawing is improving hand over fist, for much help with the illustrations.'

Why did Arthur Ransome continue to illustrate all his books with the ham-fisted Nancy's assistance? Was it a gimmick suggested by the publishers, or is Arthur Ransome secretly rather proud of his pictures? Are they his Achilles' heel? Neither answer is the right one. Arthur Ransome points out very strongly that the pictures are not, in the true sense, illustrations; they are really part of the text. He sets out deliberately to give authenticity to the stories by drawing as he thought the children would draw. The pictures are intentionally amateurish and so aim to help the reader to trust in the reality of the story. They were, therefore, an extremely interesting innovation in the technique of illustrating —one must still use the word—children's books.

Whether or not Arthur Ransome's pictures do really make many children believe that the stories are true, they have one incontrovertible asset, they encourage the reader to identify himself or herself with a particular character. Not only are the figures in the drawings often shown at a distance, but they are frequently portrayed with, so to speak, their backs to the easel.

All this would make it sound as though none of Arthur Ransome's pictures had the merit of recognisable, critical portraiture. While I am prepared to accept Arthur Ransome's insistence on the value of bad drawing, I cannot agree that his drawings *are* so very bad. . . . Nor, I think, would Frank Eyre, for one of Arthur Ransome's drawings illustrates his *Twentieth Century Children's Books*—in most distinguished company. Arthur Ransome has drawn a number of entertaining and occasionally most moving pictures; his portraits of Uncle Jim/Captain Flint are among the most endearing, particularly as the profile is that of his portrayer; his pictures of boats, quays and islands have the feel of place; and his explanatory diagrams, whether they be of ship's rigging or of pigeons-ringing-bells-in-lofts, are as clear as blueprints. His secret is hard to guess, but part of it may lie in an almost oriental emphasis on relevant shape and detail combined with a disregard of irrelevant setting.

There is a curious likeness in one of the books, *Peter Duck*, between Arthur Ransome's drawings and those of another great children's author, Hugh Lofting. Hugh Lofting, Arthur Ransome reiterates, was a 'real' artist, and his aim was that of the usual illustrator. Nevertheless, some of Arthur Ransome's pictures in *Peter Duck* are startlingly like Lofting's. In the illustration, 'The Vipers Come Aboard', for instance, one instinctively looks for Jip's, or perhaps Gub-Gub's muzzle canted over the deckhouse, and one would not be in the least surprised to see Dab-Dab's anxious beak peering out of a porthole (how like Susan she is!) or Polynesia circling angrily round the rigging.

Still, one could make too much of this curious likeness; many of Arthur Ransome's other drawings are entirely different. And so, of course, is his intention.

Illustrators of those foreign editions that do not reproduce the originals have not for the most part been very successful, but one of the American editions of *Pigeon Post* is an outstanding exception; it is illustrated most attractively, not by an American artist but—oddly enough—by Mary Shepard, E. H. Shepard's daughter.

x. Critics and Buyers

Swallows and Amazons was no immediate best seller either in its first picture-less or in its second, illustrated, edition. There were a lot of children's books on the market in 1930, and as Jonathan Cape said, the title was a sadly dull one. Besides, the author was known only as a journalist, critic and essayist, who liked fishing and sailing. And, if anyone cared to find out, he was already forty-six.

It was between two and three years, Arthur Ransome says, before the book covered his £100 advance. *Swallowdale* did not sell particularly well either, at first, and it was not until December 1932 that the tide turned. On the 2nd of that month there appeared, in *The Times*, a most enthusiastic review of his third book, published just in time for Christmas, *Peter Duck*. That same month an equally appreciative one by Hugh Walpole appeared in the *Observer*.

This incidentally healed a breach between the two men, which had existed since 1916. They first knew each other in England in 1908 and met again in Russia, when Ransome, on the *Daily News*, contradicted a report by Walpole, who was running an Anglo-Russian bureau. Rupert Hart-Davis tells the story in his *Hugh Walpole*, but does not mention the sequel. Arthur Ransome wrote to Hugh Walpole after the *Observer* review and asked if it were 'an olive branch'. 'A twig', was the reply . . . and the two were friends again.

Ever since 1932, reviews have been uniformly, almost boringly, favourable. Reviewers from David Garnett and Rosamund Lehmann, M. E. Atkinson and Mary Treadgold to the provincial paraphrases of publishers' blurbs have been unhesitating and unstinting in praise. One can almost sympathise with the *Yorkshire Post* reviewer of *We Didn't Mean to Go to Sea* (hailed by David Garnett as 'the most exciting of the series' and by Eleanor Graham as 'one of the best books for the young I had ever read') when he or she writes: 'This year I was determined not to like Mr Ransome's book best ... I surrender once more.'

Have there been no adverse criticisms? The only ones I have been able to discover have taxed Arthur Ransome with making his characters too nice—too kind and game and loyal, never cheating or squabbling. Of course no children behave so well for so long in real life, but what purpose is served by picking holes in heroes and heroines unless you do not find them credible without faults? And the chief characteristic of the Amazons, the Swallows, the 2 D's, the Death and Glories and the Eels, is that they are supremely credible and memorable. The truth is not that they have no faults but that Arthur Ransome legitimately prefers to show them to us at their nicest, which is when they are happiest and at their most interesting.

The most valuable review of Arthur Ransome to have appeared so far is perhaps the long article that was published in the *Times Literary Supplement* of June

16, 1950, under the heading 'A Contemporary Classic'. The writer concentrates on the characters rather than the plots. To my mind it is therefore all the more surprising that its author should wind up by acclaiming *Peter Duck* as 'perhaps the high-water mark'. To make amends for my admittedly rather summary and certainly prejudiced dismissal of the book, I should, I think, quote this: 'Here is something for every taste mixed together in an irresistible hotch-potch of humour and fantasy, realism and romance.' Another—and to the best of my knowledge the only other—detailed study of Arthur Ransome to date is by the Canadian Children's Librarian, Lillian H. Smith, in *The Unreluctant Years* (American Library Association, 1953). She makes an interesting analysis of *Great Northern?* and draws attention to the remarkable quality of what she finds to be Arthur Ransome's three quite distinct styles. First, she points out, there is scientific detail, described with the 'precise minuteness and the practical language of Defoe'; then there is his dialogue, 'natural and un-assuming', and finally his description of action and setting. I would agree with her evaluation of Arthur Ransome's style, but cannot see that its character changes so noticeably according to his subject matter. Colloquial simplicity and a marked economy of words are its hallmarks and can be seen, I think, even in the short extracts quoted in this monograph. He never wastes words in achieving his effect, whether it be humorous, dramatic or didactic, and it is due to this that he can slip from description to narrative to dialogue so easily and naturally.

Arthur Ransome's critical success has been complete, but what of his commercial success? He is now *Doctor* Arthur Ransome (Leeds—where his father had been Professor of History—conferred on him the degree of Doctor of Letters in 1952) and a C.B.E. (since the New Year of 1953) but have his books sold as phenomenally as those of far lesser children's writers? His publishers are reticent about exact figures, but they admit that two years ago *Swallows and Amazons* alone had sold over 210,000 copies.

This refers, of course, only to the English edition. Arthur Ransome's books have long been published in the United States, by Lippincott and Macmillan, and they have been welcomed by American children's librarians. What is more surprising, they have proved and are still proving successful in a large number of non-English-speaking countries, and have been translated into twelve foreign languages. Half a dozen have been translated into Czech; seven have appeared in French; five are available in Swedish and in German; and at least one has appeared in Norwegian, Danish, Dutch, Icelandic, Finnish, Hungarian, Polish, and Spanish.

It would be entertaining to study the variations in the different editions. In the French version of *Swallows and Amazons*, for instance, when the children are clearing up for the night on Wild Cat Island, all their activities are faithfully recorded with the exception of their brewing a final cup of tea! National and even religious feeling has demanded other alterations, not necessarily acceptable to the author. Arthur Ransome did put his foot down when one continental publisher begged him to let the Walkers and Blacketts say their prayers before they went to sleep.

Although none of the books has appeared in paperbacks, a book club did issue a limited edition of *Swallows and Amazons*. The B.B.C. has broadcast dramatised versions of the stories on sound radio, and several of them have been brilliantly read aloud by Derek McCulloch, and it is surprising that they have not yet been adapted for the theatre or the cinema, or, at any rate, for television.

xi. Children and the Writer

Although most children's books would not sell if children did not like them, not all sales can be accounted for by the number of appreciative juvenile readers. Parents and librarians are the main buyers, which may account for the continuance in print of dust-dull 'classics' that are considered salutary or at least safe. How can one gauge children's reactions to Arthur Ransome's books? There is no single certain method, but it is of some interest and value to look at the results of a competition held by Jonathan Cape in 1941. While the bombs began to fall on London, children were asked to write 250 words on their favourite Ransome. *Missee Lee* had only just been published, while *The Picts and the Martyrs* and *Great Northern?* were unwritten. There were two 'winners', a girl of nine, who plumped for *Missee Lee* (which smacks of opportunism), and a boy of eight and a half who chose *We Didn't Mean to Go to Sea*. This proves precisely nothing, but what is important is Mary Treadgold's report. 'Out of all the entries', she wrote in Cape's *Now and Then*, 'one point emerged—and that was that there was no consensus of opinion.' Evidently, children might agree with the author that the books are all volumes of the same work.

Both boys and girls have now been reading Arthur Ransome for over a quarter of a century. The Swallows and the Amazons are real to millions of people all over the world, and the Lake District, at least that part that is not William Wordsworth's, has become as much Ransome Country as Sussex is Kipling's, Belloc's or Sheila Kaye-Smith's and Dorset is Thomas Hardy's. Elinor Saltus of Arizona University was prevailed upon by her son to make a pilgrimage to meet Arthur Ransome in his own territory. In *Elementary English*, she relates how he told her that when he returned to Peel/Wild Cat Island some years after the publication of *Swallows and Amazons*, he found that the actual navigation marks had been placed on the rocks to guide boats into the hidden harbour. One other thing he told her shows the effect of the books on children. A little girl wrote to him from Africa to say that she knew he was writing about her own country because she could show him the lake near her home with every spot he mentioned located on it.

What sort of children are Ransome enthusiasts? Are they, as one would expect, predominantly middle-class? The immense sales would make one query this, even if Arthur Ransome himself did not violently contradict the notion, and produce letters from working-class schools in northern mining districts showing that whole classes of boys who could never afford the Walkers' type of holiday were fascinated by the books. I would say however that middle-class admirers are in the majority, and other readers on the decrease. This is the result, I should add, of only sketchy investigation among London librarians and booksellers and the librarian and some of the girls of a South London Comprehensive school. Middle-class children, however, seem to read him almost as avidly as ever, judging from enquiries of children at a London co-educational preparatory school.

As is the case with most authors, two or three decades after reaching the peak of their popularity, Arthur Ransome may well be read less and less for a while. But his popularity will return and return for good, because his basic stories are universal and even on the surface they do not date. One reason is that his dialogue though always colloquial is never spattered with contemporary slang.

In general the people who do not like Ransome's books are found to be those who do not share his hobbies and interests and who do not enjoy doing things for themselves. It is for this reason that many parents are mystified by the fascination the books exert over their children. The other most common cause for complaint is that the stories are too technical. And one can understand this point of view if anyone picking up *Swallows and Amazons* for the first time should find, as I did, the book opening at page 29.

'Susan had got the sail ready. On the gaff there was a strop (which is really a loop), that hooked on a hook on one side of an iron ring called the traveller, because it moved up and down the mast. The halyard ran from the traveller up to the top of the mast, through a sheave . . .'

The fact that Arthur Ransome thereupon explains what a sheave is would be small comfort to those not vitally interested.

When one is initiated into books, and even if one is a ten-thumbed landlubber, there is nothing more delightful than his obsession with the workings of things and his passion for passing on odd lore. During the course of reading the saga one can learn how to skin a rabbit, tickle a trout, catch, clean and smoke eels, use semaphore, assay copper, keep milk cool, lay patterans, burn charcoal, make a map and take flash-light photographs.

But these are incidental delights. What will remain will be the children, as secure of a place in literature as Jim Hawkins or the Bastables, Kay Harker or the Ruggles. As Marcus Crouch has written,[1] they are 'the most unselfconscious of all fictional children. Each is a highly individual person, carefully observed; each grows and develops through contact with the others and with circumstance.'

How does Arthur Ransome do it? Oddly enough, by enjoying himself—after nearly thirty years' training in writing what pleased and amused him far less. In 1937 he wrote a letter to the *Junior Bookshelf* at the request of the editor, who wanted to know 'how he did it'. His answer was to quote the one author he loved most as a child, Robert Louis Stevenson,

[1] *Chosen for Children*, Library Association, 1957.

'It's awful fun, boys' stories; you just indulge the pleasure of your heart . . .'

'That, it seems to me, is the secret,' is Arthur Ransome's comment. 'You write not *for* children but for yourself, and if, by good fortune, children enjoy what you enjoy, why then you are a writer of children's books. . . . No special credit to you, but simply thumping good luck.'

To my belief this is not the amiable white lie of a nice man refusing to discuss the agony of writing what children read with careless ease. It is the honest statement of a very great craftsman who only cares about what he makes—and who makes only what he truly cares about.

BIBLIOGRAPHY

1. CHECK LIST

*The Souls of the Streets and Other Little Papers, 1904
*The Stone Lady, Ten Little Papers and Two Mad Stories, 1905
*Highways and Byways in Fairyland, [1906]
*The Child's Book of the Seasons, 1906
*Things in Our Garden, 1906
*Pond and Stream, 1906
*Bohemia in London, 1907
*A History of Story-Telling, 1909
*Edgar Allan Poe, 1910
*The Hoofmarks of the Faun, 1911
*Oscar Wilde, 1912
*Portraits and Speculations, 1913
*The Elixir of Life, 1915
Old Peter's Russian Tales, 1916
*Aladdin and His Wonderful Lamp in Rhyme, [1919]
*Six Weeks in Russia in 1919, 1919
The Soldier and Death, 1920
*The Crisis in Russia, 1921
*The Chinese Puzzle, 1927
Rod and Line, 1929
'Racundra's' First Cruise, 1923
Swallows and Amazons, 1930. Illustrated edition, 1931. Edition with
  A.R.'s own illustrations, 1938
Swallowdale, 1931. Edition illustrated by A.R., 1938
Peter Duck, 1932
Winter Holiday, 1933
Coot Club, 1934
Pigeon Post, 1936
We Didn't Mean to Go to Sea, 1937
Secret Water, 1939
The Big Six, 1940
Missee Lee, 1941
The Picts and the Martyrs, 1943
Great Northern?, 1947
Fishing, 1955
Mainly about Fishing, 1959

*Out of print.

AMERICAN EDITIONS OF
BOOKS BY ARTHUR RANSOME

Swallows and Amazons, Lippincott, 1930
Old Peter's Russian Tales, Nelson Classics, 1935
Fishing, Cambridge University Press, 1955
'Racundra's' First Cruise, Mariner's Library, de Graff, 1958

II. BOOKS EDITED,
TRANSLATED OR WITH CONTRIBUTIONS BY
ARTHUR RANSOME
[N.B. This list is by no means exhaustive]

THE WORLD'S STORY-TELLERS
A series under the general editorship of Arthur Ransome,
each book with an introduction by him

Théophile Gautier, 1908
Ernst T. A. Hoffman, 1908
Edgar Allan Poe, 1908
Prosper Mérimée, 1908
Nathaniel Hawthorne, 1908
Honoré de Balzac, 1909
François R. de Chateaubriand, 1909
The Essayists, 1909
M. de Cervantes, 1909
Gustave Flaubert, 1909
Alphonse Daudet and François Coppée, 1909

The Book of Friendship. Edited by Arthur Ransome, [1909]
A Night in the Luxembourg, by Rémy de Gourmont, 1912. Translated, with a preface and appendix, by Arthur Ransome
The Book of Love, [1910]. Edited by Arthur Ransome
A Week, by Y. N. Libedinsky, 1923. Translated by Arthur Ransome
Down Channel, by R. T. MacMullen, 1931. Introduction by Arthur Ransome
The Cruise of the 'Teddy', by Erling Tambs, 1933. Introduction by Arthur Ransome
The Far-Distant Oxus, by Katherine Hull and Pamela Whitlock, 1937. Foreword by Arthur Ransome

Sailing Alone Around the World, by Joshua Slocum, 1948. Introduction by Arthur Ransome

The Falcon on the Baltic, by E. F. Knight, 1951. Introduction by Arthur Ransome

The Cruise of the 'Alerte', by E. F. Knight, 1952. Introduction by Arthur Ransome

The Cruise of the 'Kate', by E. E. Middleton, 1953. Introduction by Arthur Ransome

The Voyage Alone in the Yawl 'Rob Roy', by John MacGregor, 1954. Introduction by Arthur Ransome

MARINER'S LIBRARY EDITIONS
Published in America by de Graff

Sailing Alone Around the World, 1948
The Cruise of the 'Teddy', 1949
Down Channel, 1949
The Cruise of the 'Alerte', 1952
The Cruise of the 'Kate', 1953
The Voyage Alone in the Yawl 'Rob Roy', 1954